W9-CGS-592

TEAM STUDIES ON CHARACTER VOLUME 3

Rod Handley and Gordon Thiessen

ISBN 1-929478-79-8

Cross Training Publishing
(800) 430-8588

Library of Congress Cataloging in Publication Data in Progress.

I am a Christian first and last.
I am created in the likeness of God Almighty to bring Him glory.
I am a member of Team Jesus Christ. I wear the colors of the cross.

I am a Competitor now and forever. I am made to strain, to stretch and
to succeed in the arena of competition. I am a Christian Competitor
and as such, I face my challenger with the face of Christ.

I do not trust in myself, I do not boast in my abilities or believe in
my own strength. I rely solely on the power of God. I compete for
the pleasure of my Heavenly Father, the honor of Christ and
the reputation of the Holy Spirit.

My attitude on and off the field is above reproach – my conduct beyond criticism.
Whether I am preparing, practicing or playing: I submit to God's authority
and those He has put over me. I respect my coaches, officials, teammates,
and competitors out of respect for the Lord.

My body is the temple of Jesus Christ. I protect it from within and without.
Nothing enters my body that does not honor the Living God.
My sweat is an offering to my Master. My soreness is a sacrifice to my Savior.

I give my all – all of the time. I do not give up.
I do not give in. I do not give out. I am the Lord's warrior – a competitor by conviction
and a disciple of determination.
I am confident beyond reason because my confidence lives in Christ.
The results of my efforts must result in His glory.

Let the competition begin. Let the glory be God's.

Sign the Creed @ www. fca.org

CONTENTS

CONTACTING
THE AUTHORS

Rod Handley
Character That Counts
512 NE Victoria Drive
Lee's Summit, MO 64086
www.characterthatcounts.org

Gordon Thiessen
Cross Training Publishing
P.O. Box 1874
Kearney, NE 68848
www.crosstrainingpublishing.com

To contact FCA or order FCAGear
call 1-800-289-0909 or
check us out on the web at FCA.org

Team Studies on Character Volume 1, 2
are also available as well as an expanded edition,
Character that Counts for Athletes Volume 1, 2, 3

PREFACE

ow do I use this book? This book is designed to help you and your teammates build your character. In FCA we call this type of discussion a Team Huddle. It is important that you take enough time during your meetings (approximately 29-40 minutes) to go through each section of the Huddle meeting. Each week you will have the opportunity to talk about how you were able to build your character in since the previous Team Huddle. After this time of catching up, you will do a warm up to introduce this week's character. This will include an optional team building exercise. If you have time you could do this as a Huddle. You might even suggest to your coach your whole team could do this outside of the Team Huddle. After this warm up you will have the opportunity to look into the ultimate source of character building—the Bible—and discover how it might guide you as you build your character.

What is a Team Huddle? A Team Huddle is a group of athletes from a team desire to get together to discuss real life and build their character through God's principles.

How big should a Team Huddle be? This is hard to say, but generally people feel most comfortable talking and learning in a group of 10 or fewer. The bottom line is that those on your team that want to be involved should have the chance, if it is only 3 or even if it is over 20.

When should we meet? Team Huddles typically meet during the team's season. The best time to do it is before or after practice, so you are not adding another time commitment to your already busy life.

What am I committing to by being a part of a Team Huddle? The best way to get something out of the Team Huddle is to make a commitment to it. To help you do that, we have developed a Team Huddle Commitment. It isn't complicated, but it is important that you take the time to read them at the end of this introduction and then sign the commitments.

How can I get the most out of this? You will get out of this exactly what you put into it. How honest you are with yourself and the others in the Huddle will determine how much you will get out of this. It might be a stretch for some of you to risk being vulnerable and honest for the first time.

Who can lead a Team Huddle? Team Huddles are best led by someone connected with your team! It could be a player, coach, assistant coach, chaplain, etc. It is not difficult to lead a Team Huddle. You don't have to be an expert in any particular area. You simply need to want to help teammates build their character. It is important that the Team Huddle leaders are aware of FCA's Statement of Faith and are in agreement with it.

FCA's Team Huddles Commitments

- Priority--As long as you are a part of the Team Huddle, you must make the meetings a priority.
- Participation--Everyone participates, no one dominates.
- Respect--Everyone is given the right to their own opinion, and all questions are encouraged and respected.
- Confidentiality--Anything that is said in the group stays in the group and is never repeated outside of the meeting.
- Empty Chair--The group remains open to new teammates.
- Support--Permission is given to call upon each other in times of need--even in the middle of the night.
- Giving Advice--Unsolicited advice is not allowed.
- Multiplication--We agree to do everything in our power to pray that others on your team would be interested in developing their character through God's principles.

ACCOUNTABILITY

FINDING FAITHFUL FRIENDS

What did God teach you this week about character?

Nebraska volleyball player Jill McWilliams found that during her playing days for the Cornhuskers she relied heavily upon Christian friends, including the FCA women's Bible study and the Sunday night huddle meetings. "It was important to have people surrounding you who you could really talk to. It was very special to develop those types of friendships."

Accountability: Being answerable to God and at least one other person for our behavior.

1. Have you ever had the type of friendships described by Jill McWilliams? Describe the "accountability" you have had with specific players from your past.

2. Is there a specific person on this team with whom you have a high degree of accountability? How is the accountability working for you and for them?

Team Builder (Optional): Get a copy of the accountability questions from www.characterthatcounts.org Bring the questions to your next team meeting and discuss the impact of answering these questions on a weekly basis with yourself and your team.

Two men were riding a sleigh during a blizzard. They were extremely cold and terrified they would not reach safety. They came upon another traveler who had fallen in the snow. He was close to death. One of the two men on the sleigh pleaded with the other that they stop and help. The other refused. The concerned one decided to stay, even though the delay could mean his death. His companion left the two of them behind. Working feverishly, the one who stayed to help massage the unconscious man's body. After what seemed like hours of labor, the man responded and began to revive. The two men got up and walked in the snow together, the vigorous work of massage having saved them both. As they walked on, they came upon the sleigh and the man who had refused to stay and help. He was frozen to death.

The energy we spend on relationships is never wasted. Each time we stop to help a near frozen friend, we grow in our own development and character. We need each other. Together we survive. Alone, we freeze and die.

Each of us has weak spots, making us susceptible to the temptations of this world. Though some may fall because of one bad decision, most who get into trouble make a series of minor bad decisions—even decisions that go undetected—that slowly wear down their character and faith. God's Word says that we must stand firm in the faith and guard against falling away (Hebrews 5:14).

Unfortunately, some fall because they don't answer to anyone for their behavior. Choose to make yourself accountability with another person.

Many Christians mistakenly believe they can live a life of integrity without help. That attitude, however, makes us more vulnerable to sin. It ignores the biblical commands to help each other (e.g., Galatians 6:2, Eccl. 4:9-12, Proverbs 27:17).

1. Without revealing names, identify the character qualities of your three best friends. Why are they your best friends? How much do these friends really know about you?

2. What role does accountability currently play in your life? Are you satisfied with it?

3. While many people erroneously believe that accountability is bondage, in reality accountability means freedom. Why is this true?

WRAPUP

Being accountable to someone means owning up to past hurts and present shortcomings by committing to positive change. It begins with seeing the need to make changes and having the courage to make it happen with a new plan of action. Every person needs protection from self, along with a safety net. Pride is our biggest enemy. We need to reach a point where we can confess our sins and shortcomings to one another.

We're not meant to walk this journey alone. Maintaining integrity requires the encouragement of accountability. People—especially close friends—keep us pumped up. They communicate "you can do it, you can make it" a dozen different ways. At David's low-water mark, Jonathan stepped in. Right when Elijah was ready to punt, along came Elisha. Paul had Timothy, Silas and Barnabas to help him.

Here's what is against us: we are traveling through life unconnected and unexamined. We try really hard to maintain an image that we have got it all together, when in reality we don't. Inside, we are often falling apart and desperately crying for help, but we don't have the courage to talk to someone. This is exactly the reason we need to open up our hearts to others.

Accountability involves a regular check-in time to ask the hard questions and point out blind spots. Accountability also involves helping friends and teammates live up to their commitments. Through involvement in each other's lives you can really help out one another, especially when temptations hit. Teammates, coaches, pastors, counselors and our parents can help us set personal goals and then provide accountability to keep us on track.

1. React to this statement: "To live an unaccountable life is to flirt with danger." Why is this true or false?

2. Have you been corrected or criticized by a coach or a teammate recently? How did you respond? Did you hold yourself accountable or make an excuse?

3. If you needed correction in your relationship with God, who would be the one person you would want to do it? Why?

4. Is there anyone in your life asking you about real issues that you face on a daily basis? If there isn't, would you be interested in establishing an accountability relationship? Why or why not?

FINISH

This week, memorize...

"The wounds of a friend are trustworthy, but the kisses of an enemy are excessive." Proverbs 27:6

Lord, I want to assist someone today who really needs a faithful friend. Help me to....

BOLDNESS

STAND UP, STAND OUT, SPEAK OUT, SPEAK UP

Recite the Scripture verse from the last study. What did God teach you this week about character?

The headline read, "Ron Brown's boldness cost him interview with Stanford." The long time University of Nebraska assistant football coach was denied the head coaching job at Stanford because of his religious beliefs, reported the *Daily Nebraskan*. An assistant athletic director at Stanford stated, "His religion was definitely something that had to be considered." Of particular concern was his candid belief that homosexuality was a sin. Yet his well-known position was homosexuals should be loved by people just as Jesus loves them. Brown said he was

shocked at both the decision and the school's candor.

Boldness: Demonstrating the confidence and courage that doing what is right will bring ultimate victory regardless of present opposition.

1. How bold are you in sharing your religious beliefs with others?

Team Builder (Optional): Break off into pairs and share your relationship with Christ with your teammates (use the FCA "More Than Winning" tract to help you share His story and yours). After switching pairs several times, reconvene as a group and talk about what happened to you and those with whom you spoke about Jesus.

Jim is one of the nicest Christian teenagers I know. He's a varsity basketball player, he sings in the school choir, he's President of the student council and was elected Homecoming King by his classmates. He is well liked by everyone. Jim goes to church regularly; however he feels uncomfortable asking others to come with him. In fact, he really doesn't want others to know he goes to church at all. Do you know anyone like Jim?

Many student-athletes (and adults as well) find themselves busy, popular and gifted, but don't want to be known for being a Christian. They think being labeled a Christian isn't cool.

In the Old Testament, King David was famous for killing the great giant Goliath. Everyone knew his name. David could have sat back and basked in his own glory, but he chose a different path. He knew it would be unpopular to stand up for the Lord and tell others about Him, but he didn't care. David knew who gave him everything he had, and that was God Almighty!

Like Jim, many know the Lord but choose not to speak out for Him at school, on their teams and at work. Matthew 10:32-33 has some very difficult words when Jesus reminds us that if we deny Him before others, He will deny us before the Father but if we confess Him before others, He will confess us before the Father. I encourage you to stand up, stand out, speak out and speak up for Jesus Christ! While some may think you are "weird," Jesus Christ (the only One who really counts) will think far differently. You will be No. 1 in His book!

1. How are Christians viewed by your teammates and your coaches?

2. Do you shy away from sharing Christ with others? Why or why not?

3. Who do you know that needs to hear about Christ?

4. Today, how can you start taking a more public stand for Christ?

WRAPUP

Boldness is the fearless and daring courage to carry out the work God calls us to do. When Joshua was commanded to "be of good courage," he was told to have boldness—boldness to face death in battle, to speak truth from his heart and to the nation, and to do great things for God.

Almost without exception doing God's will requires risk and change. We don't like these things. We crave the familiar and comfortable. We love something we can control and get our arms around. However, that is not what God desires for us. Even though we may experience "growing pains" during these times, the closer we walk with the Lord the more He will mold us, putting boldness in our hearts to share with others what He's done in our lives. No one can argue the testimony of a changed life.

Much of what happens in our lives we simply take by faith, boldly and humbly following him. Simply put, He is the potter—we are the clay. He is the shepherd—we are the sheep. He is the master—we are His servants.

Why God does what He does, when and how He does it will often be a mystery to us. The Lord has the right to do what he wishes around us, to us and in us. As puzzling as the process may be to us, He stays with His plan. We don't need to know all the reasons. He certainly doesn't need to explain Himself. He simply asks us to boldly step out, trusting Him to guide our steps.

Doing God's will boils down to going where He wants us to go and being what He wants us to be. This means releasing personal desires and pride to follow Him. This requires faith and action. In turn, He will call us a "good and faithful servant."

1. How do you handle difficult or risky situations? What role does God play in this process?

2. Peer pressure is powerful and often dangerous. How do you react to peer pressure, especially when those pressuring you want to lead you a down a wrong path?

3. How bold are you in sharing your faith story with your teammates, friends, fans and anyone else who would listen?

4. Do you believe you are doing God's will? Would you describe yourself as being bold and humble? Why or why not?

This week, memorize…

"For God has not given us a spirit of fearfulness, but one of power, love, and sound judgment." 2 Timothy 1:7

Lord, I want to not be afraid to risk for you and even be willing to stand alone. Help me to….

CHEERFUL

BELIEVING THE BEST ABOUT YOUR TEAMMATES

Recite the Scripture verse from the last study. What did God teach you this week about character?

My daughter's 11-12 year old softball team had to be one of the worst ever. At our first practice, the girls couldn't throw, catch or hit. I whispered to my fellow coaches it would be a miracle if we won even one game. However, we agreed as coaches that our lips would only speak encouraging words; we would commit to cheerfulness at our practices and games. We decided not to worry about our regular season record, but focus on our ultimate goal: the year-end tournament.

Cheerful: Expressing encouragement, approval or congratulations at the proper time.

1. Would you describe your past and current coaches as "cheerful?" Why or why not?

2. Who is the most cheerful coach you have ever played for? How did you feel?

Team Builder (Optional): On a slip of paper, write one sentence "cheerful notes" to each of your teammates. After everyone is done, give the notes to the people you wrote about. After everyone has read his notes, comment on how these words made you feel.

At our first game, my worst fears came true. We were slaughtered 19-2 by a very mediocre team. However, we coaches found positive things to say about the girls' performance. Week after week, the losses mounted but our cheerfulness stayed constant. Of our first 13 games, we somehow managed to win two. In games #14 and #15, the girls' performance improved dramatically, and we won our last two games of the regular season.

With a 4-11 record, we decided to hold our year-end party prior to the tournament, in case we ended up losing quickly. We were seeded #13 of 16 teams. At the party, each girl was publicly affirmed in front of her teammates, family and friends for the contributions she had made during the season. It was an exciting night for each of the girls. On the way home from the party, my daughter Brooke asked me a very interesting question. She said, "Dad, who do you think we'll play in the championship game?" I almost burst out in laughter but maintained my poise and replied, "Well, I think we will play the team who finished with a 23-1 record (including winning two optional tournaments)." Brooke agreed.

Well to make a long story short, my daughter's improbable prediction became a reality as our team marched undefeated through the year end tournament-all the way to the championship. We absolutely shocked our opponents and the entire league. We were beaten in the final game, finishing second place, but I was so proud of our team, our coaches and our parents. Each person had made a commitment to be cheerful, and the results were amazing.

Being cheerful can brighten anyone's day. There are physical, psychological and spiritual rewards of cheerfulness because it is contagious. It is one of those rare treasures which is multiplied when given away.

1. How can being cheerful radically change your school, your team, your family and your community?

2. Look at each of these words: encouragement, approval and congratulations. What is the best way to incorporate these words into your life on a daily basis?

3. Is cheerfulness a "natural" or "learned" gift? What role does God play in making you cheerful?

 WRAPUP

Barnabas was known for his cheerfulness. In fact his name is translated as "son of encourager." He had a way of blessing everyone he interacted with and drawing out the best in them. In the book of Acts, Paul and Barnabas worked together well but one day they had a conflict about taking John Mark with them on a mission trip. Barnabas was willing to reach out to people who were less than perfect. The young John Mark had abandoned his ministry duties on an earlier trip to Cyprus, but Barnabas never gave up on him. Through Barnabas's encouragement, John Mark was given a second chance.

Barnabas had the unique ability to change the atmosphere around him, because he encouraged people. Whenever people were around Barnabas, their spirits were lifted, and their faith was strengthened. Guidance, help and direction is never a solo search. Growth in our lives occurs when we are surrounded and immersed in cheerful relationships. We get better and find our way in groups, not by ourselves. Positive connection with others provides guidance, encouragement and prayer support. There is lots of laughter when we are in the midst of cheerful people. Living life with others is just plain fun.

What produces cheerfulness? Cheerfulness is not the absence of trouble, but the presence of Christ. Our greatest source of cheer is eternal salvation. Because cheerfulness comes from having a genuine relationship with Christ, anything hindering that fellowship will diminish it. Jesus reminds us that cheerfulness comes by keeping the commands of the Lord (read John 15:10-13).

Jesus, remove negative attitudes and replace it with cheerfulness. Amen.

1. Go on a Bible search in the book of Acts looking for the various stories where Barnabas encouraged people. What lessons can you learn from his life? How can you become more like a Barnabas?

2. Are you considered to be a cheerful person? Why or why not? What could help you become even more cheerful?

3. Who is someone you know who needs cheered up? What specific act could you do to help them?

This week, memorize…

"Anxiety in a man's heart weighs it down, but a good word cheers it up." Proverbs 12:25

Lord, I want to exhibit a cheerful spirit to everyone. Help me to….

COMPASSION

GIVING THROUGH YOUR ACTIONS

Recite the Scripture verse from the last study. What did God teach you this week about character?

Our nation has experienced numerous tragedies in the recent past, including Hurricane Katrina. Ex-NFL quarterback Danny Wuerffel has devoted his life to serving the people of New Orleans' through Desire Street Ministries. Danny's home and ministry location were destroyed in Katrina. "I have wept over our city, thinking about the many families and children who drowned in their homes," he said. "It's an incredibly sad thing. At the same time, we've experienced times of incredible joy and vision and see an opportunity to do greater good than we've ever done before. We're very resolved and very determined and passionate about helping people."

Compassion: Investing whatever is necessary to heal the hurts of others by the willingness to bear their pain.

1. What remembrances do you have of September 11, 2001, Hurricane Katrina or other national tragedies? What acts of compassion did you hear of or participate in during these tragic events?

Team Builder (Optional): Present Red Bandannas and invite your team to join the "Fellowship of the Red Bandanna." See the website: www.redbandanna.org for details. Then, as a group determine what you can do to put your compassion into action.

As stories began to emerge from survivors of the South Tower of the World Trade Center, several mentioned a mysterious young man who stepped out of the smoke and horror to lead them to safety. They did not know this man who saved their lives, but this they did remember: Wrapped around his mouth and nose was a red bandanna.

For 76 minutes, the man in the red bandanna barked orders leading people to safety down stairwells. He said, "I found the stairs, follow me." He carried one woman down fifteen flights on his back, while leading others to safety, urged them to keep going down, then headed back up. Upstairs, a badly injured woman was sitting on a radiator when the man wearing the red bandanna came running and said, "Follow me. I know the way out. I will lead you to safety." Then he led several survivors to a stairwell that took them to safety. He was never seen alive again. Six months later, on March 19, 2002, the body of the man with the red bandanna was found intact alongside firefighters in a makeshift command center in the South Tower lobby, buried under 110 stories of rubble.

Slowly the story began to come out. Welles Crowther graduated from Boston College where he played lacrosse, always carrying his trademark red bandanna. In high school Welles was the kid who would feed the puck to the hockey team's lowest-scoring player, hoping to give his teammate his first goal. At 16 he became a junior volunteer firefighter, following in his dad's footsteps. After college he joined Sandler O'Neil and Partners, working on the 104th floor of the South Tower. He always carried change to give to street people. His dream was to become a firefighter or public servant. On 9/11/2001, at the age of 24, Welles Crowther became both, and also a hero—the "man in the red bandanna."

1. Discuss the compassion of Welles Crowther and how it compares to what you would have done if you faced similar circumstances (in your response think about Welles' compassion both before 9/11 and on 9/11).

2. What is your reaction to Danny Wuerffel's compassion?

3. Would you describe yourself as compassionate? Why or why not?

WRAPUP

Living for Christ means taking a stand to show compassion and taking active steps to draw others to God. Showing compassion is impossible without responding to needs in tangible, measurable ways.

Three men saw a wounded traveler by the side of the road. The first one must have felt sympathy (feeling sorry for people who are hurting) as he passed by. The second indicated empathy (feeling the pain with hurting people) as he came over and looked at him, but the third had compassion (doing something about the pain) as he stopped and helped him. The third man was the Good Samaritan as described in Luke 10:30-37.

Thomas Jefferson once stated, "When the heart is right the feet are swift." Real compassion begins with acts, rather than ideas. Compassion is realized by acting out Biblically— regardless of how we feel or think.

God loves a cheerful, compassionate giver who responds to the needs of others (2 Corinthians 9:7).

Compassionate people have swift feet and terrific energy! When the Israelites gave themselves and their belongings to construct the tabernacle in the wilderness, their energy was so evident they had to be told not to give anymore (Exodus 36:6-7). When the people in Jerusalem rallied around Nehemiah and rebuilt the wall, their swiftness resulted in record-breaking achievement (Nehemiah 2:17-18, 4:6, 6:15-16). In everything you do, show your compassion to those needing help by remembering Jesus' words: "It is more blessed to give than to receive."

Have you ever noticed how contagious a compassionate, generous spirit becomes? Not only do we feel great, others do as well. There is unmatched joy in learning that something you've said or done has been meaningful to another, especially when you do it without any thought of receiving anything in return. Helping others in any way— with a tangible act of kindness, a smile, a nod or a pat on the back—makes people feel better.

1. Review the Good Samaritan and Nehemiah story in detail and make any observations from these passages.

2. Think of a friend who needs your compassion right now. What could you do to help them?

This week, memorize…

"and whoever wants to be first among you must be a slave to all. For even the Son of Man did not come to be served, but to serve, and to give His life-a ransom for many." Mark 10:44-45

Lord, I want to give to those in need without regard to faith, age or nationality. Help me to....

DECISIVENESS

MAKE THE RIGHT CHOICE

Recite the Scripture verse from the last study. What did God teach you this week about character?

In Philadelphia, where fans love hard-nosed professional athletes, they are calling the play of Phillies outfielder Aaron Rowand "the catch." In May 2006, Roward ran face-first into the unpadded fence at Citizens Bank Park. He made the catch, suffering a broken nose that required surgery and left him with a splint on his nose and black-and-purple bruises under each eye. "People can think I'm dumb or whatever, but I'm here to play, and I'm here to play hard," Rowand said. His decisiveness is what you call giving up your body for the team.

Decisiveness: Learning to finalize difficult decisions on the basis of what is right, not on what's popular or tempting.

1. Decisiveness isn't just running into an outfield fence, it's also running straight into "right living." Share a time when you did the right thing when there were options to go the wrong direction. What ultimately occurred?

Team Builder (Optional): Play paintball or laser tag as a team. Afterwards discuss the role of decisiveness in the outcome of the game.

Read James 1:5-8. In this passage, notice James doesn't mess around. He goes for the jugular with a sharp scalpel. Right up front he warns us against doubting. He reminds us that in our indecisiveness, we become unstable or double-minded. Indecisiveness leaves its victims paralyzed by doubt…hesitant, hypocritical, full of words, and lacking in confidence. It is evidenced by lots of talk but no guts. James tells us that God deliberately holds back when a doubting person prays. I call that serious.

How much better to be decisive! No mumbo-jumbo. No say-one-thing-but-mean-something-else jive. No religious phony-baloney jibber jabber. Yet, be careful because decisiveness minus God is worse than indecisiveness with God. God doesn't hold back from blessing a courageous, decisive person who is fully devoted to Him.

The first step in decisiveness is choosing whom we will serve. As you'll see in the Wrapup below, when Jonathan faced a decision about facing the Philistine army, it was not a difficult choice, because he had predetermined to obey God. An indecisive person has divided desires. For example, he wants to do what is right, yet he also wants to enjoy the pleasures of this world, which last only for a short season. The minor decisions we make now paint a picture of the major decisions we will make later. The minor choices ultimately determine our character.

1. Talk about the difference between "doubt" and "decisiveness" related to your sport. How do these words and their subsequent actions impact whether you win or lose?

2. Why is decisiveness an important character quality when making life choices?

3. Share a time when you meant well, but remained indecisive and didn't follow up or follow through with something when you should have. What did you learn from this experience?

WRAPUP

While Israel's army was paralyzed with fear, Jonathan and his courageous armor-bearer decided to risk everything by trusting God in a big way. The battle noted in 1 Samuel 14 was not just dangerous, it was absurd. The only way they were going to win was if God was in it.

The Philistine army was perched high on the cliffs, making it impossible for Jonathan to approach without being spotted and killed. It would be more advantageous to be on the high ground as opposed to being low and climbing upwards. In addition, they were greatly outnumbered. It would be understandable if they had analyzed their weaknesses and questioned themselves. However, they simply asked God for a sign and when God assured them He was in it, they didn't hesitate. With decisiveness, they miraculously reached the top of the cliff and began to slaughter the Philistines. After killing twenty of their opponents, God struck with a violent earthquake and the army ran for their lives.

Not once in this story do

I see indecisiveness. The courage of Jonathan and his armor-bearer is remarkable. They faced impossible odds but never doubted. There are many times when we are asked to be decisive in our lives, believing God will prevail on our behalf. When we take a leap of faith and follow through with a decisive spirit, God will be pleased and glorified.

With the leap of faith, we see the release of God's power and strength. God sent an earthquake when Jonathan and his armor-bearer trusted and went into battle. Could God do the same thing for you? God has the power to do whatever He wishes-all we need is a decisive faith and a willingness to obey Him.

Every team faces challenges, opportunities and decisions throughout the season. How you respond to these situations will have a bearing upon your on-field and off-field performance. Assess the decisiveness of your team as a whole. Could your collective performance be improved if you executed plays with more decisiveness? Decisive individuals and teams will prove to be winners.

1. Read 1 Samuel 14:1-23. What opportunities and obstacles faced Jonathan and his armor-bearer? What was the key to their victory?

2. Share a time when you acted decisively. How did this make you feel?

This week, memorize…

"But be doers of the word and not hearers only, deceiving yourselves." James 1:22

Lord, I want to be a doer of the Word of God. Help me to….

DETERMINATION

Recite the Scripture verse from the last study. What did God teach you this week about character?

Noelle Pikus-Pace was the defending World Cup skeleton champion and first American woman to win that title. She had made a miraculous return after a speedy recovery from a broken leg that was smashed by a runaway bobsled in October 2005. Pikus-Pace returned to the sport, but her attempt to make the 2006 U.S. Olympic team in Torino fell short. Noelle did her part. Her will, determination and hard work placed her in the right place at the right time for a spot on the podium. But her sport, the system and a goofy federation governing the event played roles in preventing her from competing.

Determination: Working intently to accomplish goals regardless of the opposition.

1. What can you learn from Noelle's story?

2. Share a time when you have seen determination in action.

Team Builder (Optional): As a team, view the 92-minute documentary film "114 Days, the Race to Save a Dream" by Matt Fults. How did your team respond to the Noelle Pikus-Pace story?

You don't have to know the sport of skeleton to get the point of this story. The human drama, a dream to succeed, a push by a world-class athlete to go beyond what a normal human should have to endure-only to have a game of numbers and points end her quest.

The story is a challenge to either give up or get up. Pikus-Pace chose to get up after being hit by a runaway bobsled, steered by an inexperienced crew scared spitless. The bobsled hurtled down the track at 60 miles an hour, overshot the stop area on October 19, 2005 and plowed into Noelle, breaking her right leg.

Determined to compete in the Olympics slated to begin 114 days from the accident, Noelle had a titanium rod surgically inserted in her leg. In two weeks, she was walking. By the first week of December, she was competing in Austria, a miracle comeback. In January, she finished fifth in a race in Germany, placing ahead of every other American competitor, none of whom even made the top 10. She did this using a new sled, and she hadn't even gotten her timing down.

However, Noelle was declared unqualified to compete in the Olympics because she hadn't accumulated enough points through a season of competition scattered across the globe. Even a plea for an exemption to the International Olympic Committee citing her injury, her recovery, her increased performance capability in the span of time most people with her injury would have needed half a year just to walk, was to no avail. She was out.

Pikus-Pace will be back for the 2010 games in Vancouver, but the documentary film on her story received one review which stated, "I felt betrayed for Noelle. I wanted to find someone and knock the snot out of them. The system failed her."

1. When the smiling, bubbly Pikus-Pace finally realized she wouldn't make the team, in spite of the miracles, she broke down in tears. How do you respond when your determined efforts are shattered? Where do you go to find hope?

2. Describe a time when you, a teammate or a team showed great determination. What ultimately happened?

3. What are the keys to determination?

After one to four years at sea, the king salmon determines to head home—back to the stream where it hatched. Swimming against the fierce river currents and leaping up waterfalls, the mighty salmon increases its daily speed as it covers the hundreds of miles home. Determination gives us resolve to keep going in spite of roadblocks. No matter how daunting the task, to be determined is to see it through despite the obstacles facing us.

God's Word stresses the importance of personal determination. The Lord assures us His glory is the goal (1 Corinthians 10:31), not man's approval. Furthermore, when He tells us to love, He tells us to do it fervently (1 Peter 4:8). When maintaining a friendship, it is to be devoted (Romans 12:10). When steering clear of evil, we are told to stay away from even the appearance of it (1 Thessalonians 5:22). When seeing a brother or sister in need, we are to bear the burden sacrificially (Galatians 6:1-2), not stay at a safe distance. When it comes to my sport, I am to be disciplined (2 Thessalonians

3:7-8) and diligent (1 Thessalonians 2:9). The Scriptures abound with exhortations to go above and beyond the required call of duty-to a dedication which persists against opposition, doing my tasks with excellence.

Paul's words in Philippians 3:12-14 say press on for the goal and the prize found in Christ Jesus. God calls us to never go backward. Attempt something great for God, and do it with all your might. Few things are more rewarding than the exhilaration of achievement after wholehearted effort. The stronger the current opposing us, the sweeter the victory will be.

Christians need to persist against opposition. We are never finished until the race is done. Our adversary, the Devil, tries to discourage us constantly, but through determination, we can accomplish our goals in spite of opposition.

1. Review the passages noted above and discuss the impact of each scripture with your current team.

2. How much do you listen to "naysayers" and those who talk negative? How can you best respond with an attitude of determination?

3. Have you ever felt like quitting something but then did not? How did it make you feel to not quit? How does quitting impact other people?

This week, memorize…

"We are pressured in every way but not crushed; we are perplexed but not in despair; we are persecuted but not abandoned; we are struck down but not destroyed."
2 Corinthians 4:8-9

Lord, I want to never give up. Help me to….

ENTHUSIASM

Recite the Scripture verse from the last study. What did God teach you this week about character?

James McElwain had done everything with enthusiasm for the Greece Athena (N.Y.) High School basketball team-kept stats, ran the clock and handed out water bottles. At 5-feet-6 and considered too short to play, he opted to be the manager. McElwain, who is autistic and usually sat on the end of the bench in a white shirt and black tie, was given a new role for the last home game of his senior year when he suited up for the first time.

Enthusiasm: Expressing lively, absorbing interest in each task while giving it my best effort.

1. What role does enthusiasm play on your team(s)?

2. Who is the most enthusiastic person on your team? Describe his impact.

Team Builder (Optional): The amazing story of James McElwain has been heavily documented. Do a google search on James and download the video footage of what happened in his final ball game. Watch and discuss it with your team.

With his team way ahead, McElwain was put into the game with four minutes remaining. He poured in 20 points, including 6 of 10 three point shots, as the crowd went wild. "As soon as the first shot went in, that's when I started to get going," James said. "I ended my career on the right note. I was hotter than a pistol." He was carried off the court on his teammates' shoulders.

The inspiring story of James McElwain enthuses me. Watching the video footage of his shots, tears welled up in my eyes as I observed the response of his teammates and the crowd literally going crazy.

Enthusiasm goes a long way. Enthusiastic teams have a far better chance of achieving success than those who lack spirit and desire. A negative attitude results in defeat while those who encourage their teammates will actually inspire others toward a higher performance. Enthusiastic teams have the ability to change the momentum of games. I have seen this hundreds of times with teams at all levels.

One team I admired for years was the Pacific Lutheran University football team, out of Tacoma, Washington. Their head coach, Frosty Westering, brimmed with enthusiasm. He was able to take ordinary players and turn them into superstars. His enthusiastic approach to life transformed these young players. Frosty's approach was unconventional as he spent little time on the Xs and Os. One of his favorite football activities was taking his team to the beach and having them play a variety of relay games. His mastery as a coach was his ability to enthuse his players. Westering compiled an incredible 305-96-7 overall record (.756 winning percentage) in 40 seasons as a college coach, including four national championships.

1. Share a time when your enthusiasm inspired others. Describe what happened and the impact of your actions upon the other players.

2. Discuss each of these five statements and how each could impact your team:
   - I will put my whole heart into what I do.
   - I will treat every role on the team as important.
   - I will be an energy-giver, not an energy-drainer.
   - I will smile and seek creative ways to encourage my team.
   - I will let Jesus Christ shine through my life.

WRAPUP

To be enthusiastic is to be energized and inspired by God, giving each task our best effort. A Biblical counterpart to this word is fervent. To be fervent in spirit is to boil with heat; to be hot, as in boiling with genuine love for God and others. Another Biblical term for enthusiasm is zeal meaning excitement of mind, ardor, or fervor of spirit in pursuing or defending someone or something. Every Christian is at his best when he adds enthusiasm to his situations.

Our enthusiasm for God should exceed our sport. Praising God should be a powerful time! He wants us to glorify Him and "make a joyful noise." Isaiah 12:5-6 states that we, "Sing to the Lord, for He has done glorious things; let this be known to the entire world. Shout aloud and sing for joy." When the time comes to be with God, be enthusiastic!

We live in a world of apathy. So many people are simply existing rather than truly living. Enthusiasm deters apathy. Just knowing Christ personally should change everything about how we live. In Revelation 3:20 we are reminded of the adventure God is calling us to, "Here I am! I stand at the door and knock. If anyone hears my voice and opens the door, I will come in and eat with him, and he with me." My relationship with God, through His Son Jesus Christ, gets me out of bed in the morning. I can't wait to see what He will accomplish each and every day of my life. How about you? Are you approaching life every day with enthusiasm?

Enthusiastically embrace this fresh beginning called "today." God specializes in taking common, simple items (bread, fish, a manger, a cross, and people) and working them into miracles. You and I are the results of transformation.

1. It has been said, "No one keeps up his enthusiasm automatically. Enthusiasm must be nourished with new actions, new aspirations, new efforts, new visions." Do you believe this is true? Why? How does God fit into this quote?

2. David's enthusiastic response when the Ark of the Covenant was returned to its proper place in 2 Samuel 6 (specifically verses 14 & 15). Read this story and comment whether David acted appropriately. How do you respond when you are excited about something?

This week, memorize...

**"Let everything that breathes praise the LORD. Hallelujah!"
Psalm 150:6**

Lord, I want to increase my desire to respond enthusiastically to you. Help me to....

FAITH

GETTING INTO THE WHEELBARROW

Recite the Scripture verse from the last study. What did God teach you this week about character?

There is a story of a tightrope walker who tied his rope across a waterfall, then asked the crowd that gathered if they believed he could walk across. "Yes!" they yelled, and he did. He then asked how many believed he could walk across the falls on the rope pushing a wheelbarrow. "Yes, you can do it!" they screamed, and he did. He then asked how many believed he could do the same thing, but this time with a person in the wheelbarrow. "Oh yes! We believe it!" they exclaimed. He asked, "Which one of you will be that person?" No one responded.

Faith: Developing an unshakable confidence in God and acting upon it.

1. Describe a time when you had to place your faith in someone other than yourself. What did you learn?

Team Builder (Optional): Blindfold two volunteers and move far away. Tell the rest of the group to begin shouting as loudly as they can, all at the same time, instructing how the volunteers can reach you. Next, remove the blindfold from one person. Have him come alongside the remaining blindfolded person, not touching but quietly instructing him. Discuss how this experience relates to our faith in God.

Faith is more than saying: "I believe." To believe in what you can see requires no faith. However, believing in something you cannot see, and placing confidence in its reality as if you could see, hear, taste, touch, and smell, is genuine faith. It is having confidence to get into the wheelbarrow and trust the one pushing. Faith is to be willing to act upon belief.

One great story of faith centers on Abraham. God told Abraham He would make him and his descendants a great nation (Genesis 12:2,7). But there was a huge problem with God's promise because Abraham and Sarah had no children and were way past child bearing years. Abraham believed God and waited patiently on Him to fulfill His promise. Isaac was born when he was 100 years old and Sarah was 90.

A few years later, Abraham's faith was further tested. Hebrews 11:17-19 tells us that by faith Abraham offered Isaac as a sacrifice.

Abraham believed God could raise the dead, and figuratively speaking, he received Isaac back from death. The faith of Abraham is testimony that he believed and trusted God. As Hebrews 11:1 and 6 states, "Now faith is being sure of what we hope for and certain of what we do not see...and without faith it is impossible to please God, because anyone who comes to him must believe that he exists and that he rewards those who earnestly seek him." Just as Abraham had faith, God wants us to.

Faith is one part of the great triad: faith, hope and love. All three of these spiritual attributes look to the future through the eyes of trust. Working together, they produce the "work of faith," the "labor of love," and the "patience of hope" (1 Thessalonians 1:3). By faith, we seek to please God because we love Him.

1. Name someone you know that has an active, faith filled life with Jesus Christ. What type of influence does his/her life have upon your own?

2. What role does trust play in having faith?

3. How is faith in God lived out in your life?

WRAPUP

Hebrews 11 is often called the "Hall of Faith." It has numerous examples of men and women who took God at His word and trusted Him with the results. One example of this is Enoch, described in Genesis 5:24 as a man "who walked with God." His walk, based on faith, had remarkable results, as noted in Hebrews 11:5. Enoch pleased God, the text says, by faith. Does this mean just "intellectual faith" pleases God? No, we must have faith that diligently reaches toward God in a trust that is both hopeful and loving. "For we walk by faith, not by sight....we make it our aim, whether present or absent, to be well pleasing to Him" (2 Corinthians 5:7-9). We need to understand that "pleasing God" is realized by obedience.

The foundation of our existence is trusting God, who makes life worth living. Faith is trusting in God's providence and care. Faith is an attitude which declares, "I don't know what God is doing, but I believe that whatever it is, it's His best for my life." A person who believes does not need all the answers because he has the presence and love of Christ. God's intimate presence comforts and gives us assurance in the midst of challenges. We are like infants being held in the strong, safe arms of our parent.

Faith enables us to give up what seems good on the surface and patiently wait for what we know is best—after all, "Good things come to those who wait." Although sometimes tempted to say "yes" to something that may not be God's best, we need to faithfully choose to say "no" to anything that will compromise our relationship with God.

Have you put your full faith and trust in God, giving every area of your life to Him? Or do you just say you trust Him, refusing to get in the wheelbarrow and let Him guide you? The answers to these questions will impact your eternal home.

1. How well do you respond when life situations don't go like you've planned? What role does faith play in the midst of these challenges?

2. How would you describe your own faith in Jesus Christ? Are you certain that if you were to die tonight that you would spend eternity in heaven? Why are you sure or not sure?

This week, memorize…

"Now without faith it is impossible to please God, for the one who draws near to Him must believe that He exists and rewards those who seek Him." Hebrews 11:6

Lord, I want to be a person of great faith. Help me to….

FORGIVENESS

HAPPINESS = FORGIVING EASILY

Recite the Scripture verse from the last study. What did God teach you this week about character?

Chris Webber calls for the "timeout" and he along with his Fab Five teammates lose their opportunity to win the '93 championship game. With no timeouts left, he received a technical that cost them the game.

In every ball game mistakes are made—errant throws, dropped balls, strikeouts or falling down at inopportune moments. Few mistakes are as costly as Chris Webber's, but many professionals blow it during televised games for the whole world to see. Are these athletes not allowed to play anymore? Not at all. In fact, the player who made the mistake is often relied on immediately by his teammates to do it right on the next possession.

Forgiveness: Clearing the record of those who have wronged me, not holding their past offenses against them.

1. Have you ever blown it in a game? How did your teammates react? The fans? How did their reactions make you feel?

Team Builder (Optional): Ask each person to find a partner and share his most humiliating moment in sports (dropping a pass, shooting a game-losing airball, etc.). What bearing did it have upon the game? Have a few people share their stories with the entire group.

A number of studies reveal it is not great wealth that makes people happy, but having friends and forgiveness. Commenting on these findings in a *USA Today* article, Marilyn Elias says, "The happiest people surround themselves with family and friends, don't care about keeping up with the Joneses next door, lose themselves in daily activities, and most important, forgive easily."

An unforgiving spirit is often the last emotional fortress we yield to God. Even as Christians, we often cling to anger and bitterness, feeling that those who have wronged us should suffer for their offenses. However, when we realize how much God has forgiven us, we must compel ourselves to extend mercy (Colossians 3:12-13). Forgiving others is God's command to us and promises a life full of love, peace, thankfulness, and joy. Freely we have been forgiven; let us freely forgive.

One person said, "Forgiveness is agreeing to live with the consequences of another person's sin. Forgiveness is costly; we pay the price of the evil we forgive. Yet you're going to live with those consequences whether you want to or not; your only choice is whether you will do so in the bondage of bitterness or the freedom of forgiveness. That's how Jesus forgave you—He took the consequences of your sin upon Himself. All true forgiveness is substitutional, because no one really forgives without bearing the penalty of the other person's sin."

The forgiveness God gives is genuinely "good news." We have all made mistakes we regret, but many of us have seen blame and denial modeled as responses to sin, and these only produce more sinful behavior. God is the God of second chances....and third chances....and fourth chances....and on and on (see Psalm 86:5). The forgiveness of God washes us clean.

1. Think of a situation outside of sports when you've made an obvious mistake. How did you feel? How did others around you react? How do you think Jesus reacted?

2. Respond to this quote: "When it seems you can't forgive, remember how much you've been forgiven." Discuss the forgiveness you have been extended by Jesus Christ. How does this impact you?

WRAPUP

Why then do we forgive? Because Christ forgave us. God the Father "made Him who knew no sin to be sin on our behalf, that we might become the righteousness of God in Him" (2 Corinthians 5:21). Where is the justice? The cross makes forgiveness legally and morally right: "For the death that He died, He died to sin, once for all" (Romans 6:10).

So how do you forgive from the heart? First you must acknowledge the hurt and hate—the emotional core of your soul. Simply brushing aside the pain is something that many Christians mistakenly believe they should do because they are Christians, but that's a cover-up. We need to let God bring the pain to the surface so He can deal with it. Then healing can begin.

Ask God to bring to your mind those you need to forgive. Make a list of all who have offended you. Since God has forgiven them by His grace, you can forgive them too. For each person on your list, say: "Lord, I forgive (name) for (offenses)." Keep praying about each individual until you are sure that all the remembered pain has been dealt with. Don't try to rationalize or explain the offender's behavior. Forgiveness deals with your pain, not another's behavior. Remember: Positive feelings will follow in time; freeing yourself from the pain of the past is the critical issue.

Forgiving is tough. Letting go of past wrongs, deep resentments, or personal betrayals can seem impossible. However, counselors, psychologists and even medical doctors have seen miracles occur because of the healing power of forgiveness. It is often a crucial component to emotional recovery, family reconciliations, and in some cases, improved physical health.

1. Peter blew it when he denied Jesus three times just prior to His crucifixion. Read the entire story in Luke 22:54-62 and Matthew 26:57-75 and answer the following questions:

a. Why did Peter deny Jesus three times?

b. What impact did this have on Peter and on Jesus?

c. What ultimately resulted following this major mistake?

2. Share a time when you were extended forgiveness and how it felt to be forgiven.

3. Is there a current situation on your team or at school where forgiveness is needed? If so, make plans right now to get this situation resolved by asking your team to help you follow through with your commitment to forgive.

This week, memorize…

"And whenever you stand praying, if you have anything against anyone, forgive him, so that your Father in heaven will also forgive you your wrongdoing." Mark 11:25

Lord, I want to be quick to forgive by responding with grace to those who hurt me. Help me to….

OBEDIENCE

OBEYING IS BETTER THAN SACRIFICE

Recite the Scripture verse from the last study. What did God teach you this week about character?

Have you ever been part of a Special Olympics event? The sacrifice and obedience of the volunteers and participants is remarkable. From the volunteers, there are sacrifices of time and energy to make sure each participant is valued. With the participants, you see an amazing degree of obedience as each competitor attempts to follow the rules precisely even though he may not be able to fully comprehend them. The key for these Olympians is to compete fairly and to the best of their abilities. One parent said, "Everyone walks away as a winner at these events."

Obedience: Fulfilling instructions so that the one I am serving will be fully satisfied and pleased.

1. Have you ever participated in a Special Olympics event? If so, share your experience with the entire group.

Team Builder (Optional): Have your team volunteer to be part of a Special Olympics event. Make observations about what you learned from the day and share those at your next team meeting.

A key strategic move in baseball is when the manager asks a player to lay down a sacrifice bunt or hit a ball to the right side of the infield. This play allows a runner to advance a base while the hitter is retired. The batter's personal goals, including the desire to improve his own statistics, are not as important as obedience to the manager's directive. Players who do not follow the instructions to sacrifice will find themselves sitting on the bench.

As a Christian, to sacrifice is a willingness to say no to anything which comes in the way of our relationship with God. No sacrifice is too great when it comes to obeying. Why did Jesus Christ come to earth? He came to be obedient to His Father. Jesus Christ was the ultimate sacrifice. Even though He was completely innocent, He offered Himself as a sacrifice for others, including His enemies. He became our substitute, placing our sin directly on Himself, taking it

to the cross. It was a sacrificial act of obedience by Jesus Christ, the Son of God (Philippians 2:5-11).

While Jesus was completely obedient, King Saul revealed his disobedience. The Lord's instructions to Saul in 1 Samuel 15 were very specific. He was to totally destroy the Amalekites. Nothing, including livestock, was to be spared. Saul killed their army, but he spared King Agag. He also kept the finest livestock, rationalizing his disobedience by sacrificing them to the Lord. When Samuel heard what Saul had done, he was both angry and heartbroken. "Why did you not obey the Lord?" he questioned Saul. "I thought God would be pleased with my sacrifices," Saul whispered. "God wants your obedience rather than your sacrifices," Samuel answered angrily. Saul pleaded for forgiveness but this act of disobedience was the last straw—God rejected him as king over Israel.

1. Comment on the following quote: "Our attitude and actions each play a part in obedience." Why is this true?

2. Is your team obedient to the direction of your coach? Why or why not? What are the consequences of disobedience?

3. Discuss the ramifications of living obediently in the context of your coach, your teammates, at home and with God.

WRAPUP

Saul's story is a dramatic and tragic account of the consequences of disobedience. His life was a series of compromises. While it may seem these are "little compromises" God takes disobedience very seriously. I call it being "One Degree Off." While one degree may seem miniscule initially, as the lines are extended, the gap becomes wider. One person described it this way, "If you were to fly a plane from New York City to Sydney, Australia and you were one degree off, you would land hundreds of miles away from your target destination, somewhere in the Outback." This is what happens when we live "One Degree Off." We will stray from God's path.

In what ways are you compromising and being disobedient? In Saul's case, he thought partial obedience would satisfy God, but from this story we learn that full obedience is the only way to please Him. Today, we find it easy to give up sins which make us feel depressed and weak but how do you handle sinful areas which you find fun, entertaining and pleasurable? For example, we know we shouldn't date an unbeliever, but he or she is just so good looking. We know we shouldn't gossip with our friends, but it's so fun when you have juicy news to spread. God never said we could just keep the "fun sins." He requires us to rid ourselves of every sin without compromise.

Saul deceived himself that he was pleasing God while being disobedient. It's easy for us to do the same. God, through his Word and the conviction of the Holy Spirit must be the final authority over what is right and wrong in our lives. There are times when God may use a coach or a teammate to challenge us in an area that needs to be addressed. It's never fun

or easy to be made aware of sin, but it is necessary if you want to avoid sin's consequences—which are even more painful. Search your heart carefully and ask God to help you be obedient in all areas of your life.

1. Read 1 Samuel 15:1-26 to get the full story of Saul and his disobedience. Unpack the story and discuss why this was a great disappointment to God.

2. John 14:15 says, "If you love Me, you will keep My commandments." In what ways are you compromising and being disobedient to God and His Word? What do you need to do to change?

This week, memorize…

"There is a way that seems right to a man, but its end is the way to death." Proverbs 14:12

Lord, I want to be aware of little compromises which can get me sidetracked. Help me to….

PASSIONATE

Recite the Scripture verse from the last study. What did God teach you this week about character?

On June 19, 1986, Maryland basketball star Len Bias died of cocaine intoxication two days after being selected by the Boston Celtics as the second overall pick in the NBA draft. His mother, Lonise Bias, had no idea he was using the drug. Since his death, Lonise has been on a passionate crusade conducting workshops and seminars around the country in an effort to stop drug abuse among our nation's youth. She launched the campaign over 20 years ago to cope with her loss and to help parents avoid a similar tragedy. "I have seen a lot of good come out of his death. I believe Len's death helped turn the situation around involving drugs. Len lost his life to help save others."

Passionate: Having intense, powerful or compelling emotions and feelings towards others or something.

1. Lonise Bias also said, "If Len would have lived he would have entertained you. But in death, he brought life." How can this be true?

Team Builder (Optional): Mel Gibson's movie, "The Passion of the Christ" is a powerful picture of the passion of Jesus as He died on the cross. As a team, watch this movie and discuss the passion of Jesus Christ.

I love to be around people who are passionate about life and athletics. People with passion have energy and an attitude which brings out the best in others. Andy Andrews said, "Passion is a product of the heart. Passion is what helps you when you have a dream. Passion breeds conviction and turns mediocrity into excellence! Your passion will motivate others to join you in pursuit of your dream. With passion, you will overcome insurmountable obstacles. You will become unstoppable!" Throughout my lifetime, I have had the privilege of being around people of passion, and I have always benefited greatly from them. While I have never met Lonise Bias, I know I would like her because she is passionate about helping people.

To see passion personified, we need only to look at Jesus Christ. The word "passion" comes from a Latin word meaning "suffering." The suffering He endured could not have been any more horrific. Even before the Roman guards captured Him in the Garden of Gethsemane, He was sweating drops of blood (Luke 22:44). He literally took the sins of the entire world, past, present and future, upon Himself. The beatings, the taunts from the crowd, the gruesome walk on the Viva Delarosa to Calvary and the nails driven into His hands and feet, were all part of God's supreme plan to save mankind. His passion for you and me was what gave Him the will to go the cross for our sins.

One of the most stunning statements Jesus ever made was about His own death and resurrection is found in John 10:17-18. Jesus chose to die. His Father ordained it and He embraced it.

1. Besides Jesus, who is the most passionate person you know? What do you think fuels their passion?

2. What are you passionate about?

3. Read John 10:17-18. How does the passion of Jesus impact you?

WRAPUP

John Piper said, "Because of this unparalleled passion, God raised Jesus from the dead. It happened three days later. Early Sunday morning he rose from the dead. He appeared numerous times to His disciples for forty days before His ascension to heaven (Acts 1:3). Jesus finished the work God gave him to do, and the resurrection was the proof that God was satisfied." His resurrection proved we were now free from the bondage of death. We are now fully reconciled to God.

The passion of Jesus Christ is the most important event in history and to this day it is still the most explosive topic on planet earth. His death and resurrection is the centerpiece of God's entire plan. The apostle Paul recognized the importance of these events when he penned his words as noted 1 Corinthians 15:13-19 (read these verses).

The apostles, who saw Jesus after his death and resurrection, clearly knew based on firsthand evidence that He was alive. Thus every one of them willingly died for Him because they knew the truth of His passion. In fact, His passion became their passion. Without this assurance, they would have scattered in many directions trying to save their own skin. Instead, they were martyred themselves, thus perpetuating the truth about Jesus Christ.

Years ago during my senior year of high school, I was impacted greatly by a sophomore on my football team. He understood and lived out the passion of Jesus Christ. When he practiced or played, he imagined Jesus Christ sitting in the bleachers watching his every move. His passion to perform for Jesus Christ was his only motivation. He gave effort which was beyond the entire team. I saw this young athlete work, sweat and

compete for the glory of God. This sophomore's passion changed me and our entire team.

How about you? Are you willing to lay everything out on the field because Jesus Christ laid it all out for you? If so, your passion will impact people for eternity.

1. Read the crucifixion story found in the Gospels (Matthew 27-28 is one of the accounts). Discuss this event and why it was deemed important by the authorities to claim the body was stolen. Why the cover-up? Why is this story the most important historical event of all time?

2. What is something that you are passionate about? Why?

This week, memorize…

"Flee from youthful passions, and pursue righteousness, faith, love, and peace, along with those who call on the Lord from a pure heart." 2 Timothy 2:22

Lord, I want to passionate about you and for you. Help me to….

RESPECT

TREATING OTHERS WELL

Recite the Scripture verse from the last study. What did God teach you this week about character?

High school football coaches in Connecticut will have to be on their best sportsmanship in the 2006 season or risk suspension. New rules passed by the state have adopted a "score management" policy that will suspend coaches whose teams win by more than 50 points. It is now considered an unsportsmanlike infraction and will result in a one-game suspension. By some, it is dubbed the "Jack Cochran rule," after the New Long High School football coach logged wins of more than 50 points last season-including one 90-0 margin. One person commented, "It's all a matter of respecting your opponent and the game." Cochran acted with little regard for the opponents his team faced.

Respect: Honoring and esteeming another person due to deep admiration.

1. Have you ever been part of a team that was on the winning or losing side by a large margin? Describe how it felt.

2. Would it impact your team if your state enacted the "Jack Cochran rule"?

Team Builder (Optional): Go through your local newspaper finding any recent games with a 50+ point margin and determine how long key players remained in the game before the reserves were inserted. Determine an action step for your team and for your opponents.

"Simply put, we did not respect them, and you cannot do that." These were the words of Vladislav Tretiak, goaltender for 1980 USSR ice hockey team, commenting after losing to Team USA in the 1980 Winter Olympics, "The Miracle On Ice." This win by Team USA is considered one of the biggest upsets in the history of sports and is partially attributed to Team USSR not respecting Team USA or giving them even a remote chance of winning.

Respect is how you treat and regard others. It is your regard for the worth and dignity of every human being. Many people refer to respect as "The Golden Rule" which comes from Matthew 7:12 and Luke 6:31. Lawrence-Lightfoot said, "Respect is not something one can imitate, but something one must embody...a person has a disposition to act with respect, it is only in the individual acts of respect that the quality becomes actual....respect is maintained by the respectful acts of individuals."

Many people argue that respect in sports is exhibited in how an athlete approaches the game and his opponents. While this is partially true, respect entails much more than that. Within athletics there should be respect for self, teammates, opponents, fans, coaches, and referees. Examples of respectful behaviors include shaking hands, helping a teammate or opponent up, and listening to your teammates, coaches and referees. It also means being on time to practice, being prepared, obeying a coach's instructions, submitting to those in authority and giving one's best effort in practice and games.

Behaviors that show lack of respect include taunting, trash talking, yelling at a coach or referee, cheating, running up the score against an inferior opponent, and treating ones opponent as a mere means to the goal of victory.

1. Review the Golden Rule. Why is this rule an important principle especially in sports?

2. Does your team respect teammates, opponents, fans, coaches and referees? Why or why not? Be specific with your response.

3. Is your team respected by others? Why or why not?

WRAPUP

Sport participants' behaviors are often instinctive and instantaneous. Sports are highly emotional, physical, stressful, and involve situations that are often far too aggressive. Time for moral reasoning and common sense processing frequently does not exist in sports. Many times athletes react quickly without thinking. There are times these responses and reactions come with regret. Yet, each reaction reveals another facet of an athlete's true character.

Ultimately a person must be responsible for his actions because there are consequences for negative behavior. By respecting oneself and following a set of pre-established values, both personal and team, athletes can control themselves and their behaviors. If a Christian athlete's behavior does not reflect his character, then this person is not being true to his values, and therefore lacks character. An individual's attitude and beliefs are important, but our actions reveal the truth about who we really are.

One of the ways a young person can be blessed by God is found in the 10 Commandments (Exodus 20:1-17). God says in the fifth commandment to "honor your father and your mother." In essence, the command is to respect them. A majority of teens falsely believe their parents are "out of touch" and have no clue about anything. Years later, many of them are amazed at how smart their parents became once they moved out of the home. God has uniquely placed your parents in a position of authority and God has called you to respect and honor them-period! My encouragement is to follow God's commands by honoring your parents.

In addition, God also establishes and oversees all authority as noted in Romans 13:1-7. We need to understand this important principle as it applies to our sports, our schools and our communities.

1. Read Exodus 20:1-17 and Romans 13:1-7. Note the different passages where respect is commanded by God. Are there any exceptions stated?

2. How does a person give and gain respect?

3. Are you respected by others? Why or why not?

4. Examine your behavior in recent games. Have your quick reactions reflected respect of self and others?

This week, memorize…

"…submit yourselves to your masters with all respect, not only to the good and gentle but also to the cruel." 1 Peter 2:18

Lord, I want to make the Golden Rule one of my life principles. Help me to….

SERVANTHOOD

DOING WHATEVER IT TAKES

Recite the Scripture verse from the last study. What did God teach you this week about character?

All 20 of the Louisiana State University Tiger athletic teams had representatives, both coaches and players, spending time assisting the Red Cross with Hurricane Katrina victims. LSU men's basketball standout Glen "Big Baby" Davis was among the volunteers at the Maravich Assembly Center triage unit. As dozens of ambulances lined up outside the arena with scores of injured victims, Davis was inside, working until 3:00 a.m. doing everything he could. He unloaded trucks. He wheeled in patients and even assisted doctors with a severely injured man on the floor of the arena.

Servanthood: Caring for and meeting the needs of others before caring for self.

1. Describe a time when you have served and/or been served? How did it make you feel?

2. Who are people we should serve? Why?

Team Builder (Optional): As a team, find a place where you can serve your community. Perhaps it is serving a meal to the homeless, cleaning up a home or _____ (be creative). Now, just do it!!

Across campus, LSU equipment manager Greg Stringfellow and his staff washed linens and clothes for victims who needed clean sheets or a change of clothes at the shelter. As the clothes came out of the dryers, the volleyball, women's soccer, softball and gymnastics teams were all there to fold the clothes. In all, Stringfellow and the students washed an estimated 14,000 pounds of laundry in two days.

The Tiger football team spent time with families who were displaced from their homes. "I just don't know what to say. It's such a horrible deal but if there is any small, miniscule way that we can help people or put a smile on somebody's face, we will try to do it," said senior center Rudy Niswanger. "We had a Red Cross lady come up to us and talk about what a great thing it was that we were there. It really made me think that we were only there for 45 minutes signing things and passing out shirts and this lady is going to be there 24 hours a day for the next three weeks. And she's talking about what a great thing it is we are doing? It really makes me think about what she is doing and what the contributions of people like that are making. This definitely shows that football is just a game. It is not nothing comparable to what these people are going through."

The LSU women's soccer team, already a week into its season, also managed to volunteer despite having practice earlier in the day. "We filled out forms and helped fax," LSU soccer standout Tara Mitnick said. "But more than anything, we just listened to people. We listened to their stories, what they had to say. We just gave them someone to talk to."

Servanthood isn't reserved for those who are skilled or gifted for service-servanthood is a duty for all Christians. Our role model is Christ himself who came "not to be served, but to serve" (Matthew 20:28).

1. What is God's perspective on serving?

2. Why is servanthood so vital to a community? What role do you play in serving others?

3. What is an area of service that God has been prompting you to? Have you responded to His call?

WRAPUP

Chuck Swindoll in "Improving Your Serve" gives three dynamic statements which capture the essence of what every believer in Christ should pursue in serving:

1) Transparent Humanity: No one is perfect!! If anyone was close, it was Paul. Yet, he didn't hide his humanity (see Romans 7). He openly declared his true condition and the battle waging inside of him. He had needs and admitted them. Servants are real people....just like you and me.

2) Genuine Humility: A true servant humbles himself in order for God to get all the credit, glory, honor and praise. There is less of self and more of God. Some revealing traits of humility include: A non-defensive spirit when confronted; a willingness to be accountable; a teachable spirit; an authentic desire to help others; always looking for ways to give; and his attitude is: "nothing to prove and nothing to lose."

3) Absolute Honesty: Honesty has a beautiful and refreshing simplicity. There are no ulterior motives or hidden meanings. It is an

absence of hypocrisy, duplicity, manipulation and political games.

FCA Vice-President Dan Britton states, "In the athletic world, everyone struggles to some degree with the "me first" mentality. We buy into the lie that we are better than others because of our giftedness in athletics. So are we consumed with self or with serving? When serving, we need to have intentionality (Plan it!), intensity (Seize it!) and intimacy (Feel it!). The passion for serving must come from the heart."

On and off the field, we need to be radical about serving. Can you imagine if thousands of coaches and athletes across the country got passionate about serving?

Why shouldn't that revolution begin with you?

1. Look up the following passages on serving and discuss them as a team (Deuteronomy 10:12; John 13:1-17; Galatians 5:13).

2. Why is it hard to be passionate about serving? What gets in the way?

3. What part(s) of your life reflect the "me first" mentality? Identify, confess and ask for forgiveness.

4. Will you be one of those who are passionate about serving? If so, what is one practical way you can serve today?

This week, memorize…

"Render service with a good attitude, as to the Lord and not to men." Ephesians 6:7

Lord, I want to follow the example of Jesus Christ by being a servant. Help me to….

TOLERANCE

Recite the Scripture verse from the last study. What did God teach you this week about character?

In 2006, the Northwestern (IL) women's soccer team was suspended indefinitely after photographs of alleged hazing appeared on the Internet. The team issued an apology for the "negative attention, press and controversy" it caused the school. "We fully accept responsibility for our behavior and understand the magnitude and severity of the current situation," the team said in a letter that appeared in the school newspaper. They went on to say, "this incident does not reflect the values, integrity and qualities we seek to embody. We never foresaw that what began as a well-intentioned night of team unity and celebration would have such severe consequences."

Tolerance: Learning to accept others as valuable individuals regardless of their maturity.

1. Hazing and other acts of immaturity can have harmful consequences on individuals and teams. What are some consequences which occur when tolerance isn't exhibited?

Team Builder (Optional): Throw a team party void of alcohol, drugs, hazing and any other acts which could cause an incident affecting individual players, your school or community. After the party, discuss how everyone felt about exhibiting tolerance.

We live in a society which strives to be "politically correct." There are certain words and phrases which can't be used for fear of how people will react and respond. Today, I want to ask you a question, "Is Christianity tolerant?" The answer is, "Yes and no." How is that for being "politically correct"? Let me explain:

NO - Jesus himself was intolerant. He clearly tells us in John 14:6 that He is the way, the truth and the life and no one can come to the Father except through Him. In Acts 4:12 we are told there is no other name under heaven other than Jesus by which a person can be forgiven of his sins. It is intolerant to say there is only one true God as Jesus said in John 17:3. Jesus was intolerant when He said He is the one who reveals God to people (Luke 10:22). Jesus was extremely intolerant of religious hypocrisy when He condemned the religious know-it-alls, calling them deceivers (Matthew 23:25-26). Jesus was intolerant when He threw the moneychangers out of the Temple (John 2:13-16). Jesus was also intolerant of hatred (Luke 6:27), ignorance (Matthew 5) and prejudice (Luke 10:30-37). In addition, Christianity is intolerant of serving false gods and false prophets. Christianity is intolerant because its founder, Jesus, was intolerant.

YES - Christianity is also tolerant. It teaches forgiveness (Matthew 18:21-22), patience and kindness (Galatians 5:22-23) and honesty and wholesomeness (Philippians 4:6-8). Jesus taught us to love and to be examples of truth to the world. While he was intolerant of pride, rebellion, sin, covetousness, adultery, lying, cheating, stealing, fornicating and murder, yet at the same time He demonstrated great love and patience with those who were guilty of all these things. God's intolerance for sin does not negate His love for people. God desires to help us avoid sin fleeing from temptations, bringing about holiness, peace and righteousness in our lives (Hebrews 12:10-11).

1. How do you view Christianity relating to tolerance and intolerance?

2. How can Christians show more tolerance and yet not be guilty of violating God's truth?

3. How tolerant are you personally?

WRAPUP

The issue of whether or not Christianity is tolerant lies in who Jesus is, what He claimed, and what He did. If what Jesus said and did is true, then Christianity is both tolerant and intolerant. Christ's message boils down to the truth of His life.

It is true Jesus lived. It is true Jesus walked on water (Matthew 8:26-27). It is true Jesus healed the sick (Matthew 8:5-13). It is true Jesus calmed a storm with a command (Mark 4:39). It is true Jesus raised the dead (Matthew 9:25; John 11:43-44). It is true Jesus claimed to be God (John 5:18; 8:24; 8:58—see Exodus 3:14). It is true Jesus was killed on a cross (Luke 24:20). It is true Jesus rose from the dead (Luke 24:39; John 20:27). These are not feeble claims made by crazy people who wanted to gain power and fame. These are the truths of Christ and of those who followed Him, suffered for Him, and died for Him.

Either Christianity is wholly true or it is not. Either Jesus performed miracles or He did not. Either Jesus rose from the dead or He did not. Based solely and completely on who Jesus is and what He did, Christianity is the truth and by necessity all other religions that disagree with Jesus are wrong. If Christianity is false, then Jesus was not God and everything He said and did is a total fraud. But, if He is who He claims, then Christianity alone is true.

So how does your team practice tolerance? I encourage you to speak the truth in love by being real and caring. Being antagonistic, prideful, manipulative and telling people they are going to hell isn't a way to communicate God's love. Be intolerant of the world's view of God and values. Cling to your faith and don't give in. However, like Christ, you can be intolerant but also tolerant at the same time without compromising godly standards including honesty, responsibility, thoughtfulness, punctuality, self-control, patience, purity, compassion, diligence, etc. May your response to others be in line with today's memory verse (see below).

1. Look up all the Scripture noted in this lesson (there's a ton of it). Was Jesus a liar, a lunatic or the Lord?

2. How can I stand my ground for my beliefs, yet minister effectively to those around me?

This week, memorize...

"But set apart the Messiah as Lord in your hearts, and always be ready to give a defense to anyone who asks you for a reason for the hope that is in you. However, do this with gentleness and respect, keeping your conscience clear... ." 1 Peter 3:15-16

Lord, I want to exhibit Your tolerance. Help me to....

VISIONARY

SEEING YOUR DREAMS FULFILLED

Recite the Scripture verse from the last study. What did God teach you this week about character?

At 5-foot-6 and 165 pounds, his chances of playing football for Notre Dame were slim to none. But Rudy Ruettiger had envisioned himself playing for the Fighting Irish since he was a boy, and he was willing to pay the price to make it happen. In 1974 he walked on and made the practice squad, and in 1975 got to dress and play in the final game of the season. Rudy says, "Along the way the journey will be full of struggle, but I learned that the greater the struggle, the greater the victory!"

Visionary: Dreaming not inhibited by the unknown.

Looking beyond problems by creating successful solutions.

1. What are your dreams and aspirations for sports and life in general?

2. What are you doing today to help pave the way for your vision?

Team Builder (Optional): Rent the movie "Rudy" and watch it with your team. Talk about the vision he had and how his determination to see that vision come true resulted in an amazing story.

I have heard that 90 percent of all millionaires have a personal mission or vision statement, yet fewer than three percent of all other individuals have one. A vision statement helps people discover what drives them, where their passions lie and what brings energy and focus. It is a compass or a road map with a plan for lifelong learning and personal development. It needs to be continually prayed through and evaluated.

One practical step you can take as an individual or a team is to develop a vision statement. The most effective statements are one sentence long, can be understood by a 12-year-old and can be recited at gunpoint. After this statement is prepared, you can develop a series of goals to establish a thorough game plan. This will help give you direction, purpose and focus on what is really important.

God has uniquely gifted you with the personality, talent and experience to accomplish more than you can even dream or imagine (Ephesians 3:20). Today, let us understand that we must act on our God-given vision. Author and pastor Andy Stanley reminds us, "If God has birthed a vision in your heart, the day will come when you will be called upon to make a sacrifice to achieve it. And you will have to make the sacrifice with no guarantee of success." We know that the sowing of great sacrifices is required for the reaping of great rewards.

Stanley puts it this way: "Vision requires the commitment of a parachutist. You don't 'sort of' parachute. You are either in the plane or in the air." I challenge you to take the risks and make the sacrifices needed in order to move toward the vision God has put in your heart.

1. Do you have a personal mission or vision statement? If so, share it with your team. If not, commit to creating one prior to your next meeting.

2. Does your team have a vision statement? If so, review your statement and talk about what it means to each person. If you don't have a team statement, work together on establishing one and then identify specific goals which will help you achieve the vision statement.

WRAPUP

Years ago, I heard former professional baseball player, Harold Reynolds speak on "vision" and he shared several important truths including:

* Have a vision: Habakkuk 2:2 says to write your vision down, so you'll recognize it when it unfolds. We have to know our reason for living.

* Commit to the vision: Just like focusing a camera, making a commitment helps focus our vision, making it clearer to us. It helps to begin with the end in mind which allows us to see the outcome before others do.

* Don't get distracted or discouraged from the vision. Jesus came so we could have life, but Satan wants to steal, kill and destroy (John 10:10).

* Stay on the right path because it builds confidence. Proverbs 4:18 says, "The path of the righteous is like the first gleam of dawn, shining ever brighter till the full light of day." The further you go, the clearer things will get.

* Allow the vision to mature. Sometimes we give up too fast. As Christians, we need to have patience. Visions take time.

* Develop good work habits. Excellence in any area of life demands good work habits...whether prayer, Bible reading or baseball. I worked on my swing and developed good habits in baseball, and even though I still have rough times, those good baseball habits will get me through.

* Run through the tape. You have all seen sprinters lean into the tape at the end of the race. In the spiritual race of life it's not how well you start but who endures to the end and leans to the tape (1 Corinthians 9:24-25).

* Remember the vision because the vision keeps you alive. Proverbs 29:18 reminds us that when there is no vision, we perish.

The process of writing a vision statement and establishing goals can be one of the most valuable exercises you will ever go through. Try it.

1. Review the following passages (Genesis 12:1-5; Mark 1:16-20; Mark 2:1-5 and 2 Corinthians 11:16-27) and discuss the risks and sacrifices required.

2. Review the list of items mentioned by Harold Reynolds and comment on each statement.

3. Reflect on the vision God has currently put on your heart. What sacrifices are necessary? Are you willing to make them?

This week, memorize...

"Without revelation (vision) people run wild, but one who keeps the law will be happy." Proverbs 29:18

Lord, I want to see my/our vision accomplished. Help me to....

WORSHIP

DOING IT IN SPIRIT AND TRUTH

Recite the Scripture verse from the last study. What did God teach you this week about character?

At the 1924 Paris Olympics, Eric Liddell dropped out of his best event, the 100-yard dash, because qualifying heats were held on a Sunday. Instead, Liddell entered himself in the 400-yard dash. During the Sunday heats, he preached a sermon at a Paris church. The 400-yard dash was not what he had trained for, but Liddell finished five yards ahead of his nearest competitor, setting a world record of 47.6 seconds. He attributed his win to God. After his triumph at the Olympics, Liddell moved to China as a missionary, following in his parents' footsteps. The critically-acclaimed and Oscar winning 1981 film, Chariots of Fire, is based in part on the story of Eric Liddell.

Worship: Honoring God reverently

1. Where do you go to worship the Lord?

2. How would you define worship? How do you worship?

Team Builder (Optional): Do a google search on Eric Liddell and discover the depth of his story and his character. Discuss as a team ways you can worship the Lord.

Is worship confined to a building or a structure? Is it possible to worship God Almighty anywhere, anytime, anyplace? Several memorable quotes from Eric Liddell are noted in Chariots of Fire. In one scene, Eric says, "Then where does the power come from, to see the race to its end? From within." Later he says, "I believe God made me for a purpose, but he also made me fast. And when I run I feel His pleasure." Eric Liddell worshipped God through his sport and later he worshipped the Lord by serving as a missionary until his death.

According to Rick Warren, "The heart of worship is surrender. In today's culture we are taught to never give up and never give in-so we don't hear much about surrendering. If winning is everything, then surrendering is unthinkable." But surrendering to God, which brings God pleasure, happens when you give yourself completely to Him. It means giving God all of your life-sports, academics, relationships, career, etc. Surrendering to God is not being passive or lazy. It isn't suppressing your personality. C.S. Lewis said, "The more we let God take us over, the more truly ourselves we become-because he made us."

You know you are surrendered to God when you rely on Him to work things out as opposed to manipulating others, forcing your agenda or controlling situations. As Joshua approached the biggest battle of his life (Joshua 5:13-15), he encountered God, fell in worship before Him, and surrendered his plans. That surrender led to a stunning victory in Jericho. This is the paradox: Victory comes through surrender. Surrender doesn't weaken you; it strengthens you.

1. How do you view the words "surrender" and "winning"? Can they occur simultaneously? How can you surrender to win in your life?

2. Based on the information above, what is your view of worship?

3. How do your actions in practice and on game day compare to your actions during worship?

WRAPUP

Eric Liddell was a man who totally surrendered his life to God (James 4:7). He was willing to accept anything God did in his life whether it was running through the tape on the race track or serving in China. This is true worship!!

In contrast to Eric's lifestyle of worship, we don't often see this example in the real world. As you read the following story, consider how this ties to worship.

The world championship hung in the balance when Briana Scurry, the American goalkeeper, strode to the goal line at the Women's World Cup. Scurry had picked out her victim, the third Chinese player to take a penalty kick in the shootout.....it was one thing to choose which opponent was most likely to be weak. It was another thing for Scurry to choose her tactics. By her own admission, Scurry decided to improve her chances by ignoring the penalty kick rules. In a quick and practiced move, Scurry bolted two steps forward-a violation-and cut off the angle for Liu Ying, her opponent. With superb reflexes, Scurry then dove to her left and tipped Liu's shot wide of the goal. That one stop gave the U.S. the championship. Scurry's position was clear soon after the game when she told The *Los Angeles Times:* "Everybody does it. It's only cheating if you get caught."

The lessons you have read throughout this book have all prepared you for this final chapter on worship. To worship is to "honor God reverently." He is the object of our worship. He makes it worth it all. Our one goal in life should be to worship Him and to bring Him glory, honor and praise. He demands it, and He deserves it. The Brianna Scurry story is a smack in the face of worship. Is life all about trying to gain a competitive edge, winking at sin when you don't get caught? The reality is that we all will stand before God someday and give a full accounting of our life to Him. He should be our only audience. We should view our lives as an opportunity to worship Him alone. My encouragement to you is to worship Him in spirit and in truth (John 4:24). Perform solely for Him. Use your God-given talents to bring Him glory. Sink deep into His Word and let Him guide you.

1. Describe what it means to play to an "Audience of One." Refer to Colossians 3:17 and 23.

2. Read Psalm 33 and 98. How do these chapters exhort us to worship?

This week, memorize…

"God is spirit, and those who worship Him must worship in spirit and truth." John 4:24

Lord, I want to worship you in spirit and truth. Help me to….

FELLOWSHIP OF CHRISTIAN ATHLETES

FCA's Vision

To see the world impacted for Jesus Christ through the influence of athletes and coaches.

FCA's Mission

To present to athletes and coaches, and all whom they influence the challenge and adventure of receiving Jesus Christ as Savior and Lord, serving Him in their relationships and in the fellowship of the Church.

FCA Ministries (The 4 C's)

Coaches Ministries

At the heart of FCA are coaches. Our role is to minister to them by encouraging and equipping them to know and serve Christ. FCA ministers to coaches through Bible studies, staff contacts, prayer support, discipleship and mentoring, Behind the Bench, resources, outreach events, national and local conventions, conferences and retreats.

Campus Ministries

The Campus Ministry is initiated and led by student-athletes and coaches on junior high, high school and college campuses. The programs of the Campus Ministry include Huddles, Team Bible Studies, Chapel Programs, TeamFCA Membership, *One Way 2 Play - Drug Free!* and Special Events.

Camp Ministries

Camps are a time of inspiration and perspiration for athletes and coaches to reach their potential by offering comprehensive athletic, spiritual and leadership training. The types of Camps are Sports Camp, Leadership Camp, Coaches Camp, Youth Sports Camp, Partnership Camp and Team Camp.

Community Ministries

The non-school based FCA ministries reach the community through partnerships with the local churches, businesses, parents and volunteers. These ministries not only reach out to the community, but also allow the community to invest in athletes and coaches. Community Ministries include: Stewardship Ministries,

Adult Ministries, Sport-Specific Ministries, Urban Initiatives, Clinics, Product and Resource Development, and Professional Athlete Ministries.

FCA MINISTRY FUNDAMENTALS

FCA Ministry Fundamentals are Share Him, Seek Him, Lead Others and Love Others. The Ministry Fundamentals are the simple expression of what we are trying to accomplish. They are the foundations of all we do as a ministry. We believe that God has given us a ministry of evangelism to present (Share Him) the saving knowledge of Christ on the field, in the locker room and the hallways. We believe that once a person has come into a relationship with Christ there is the challenge (Seek Him) to be discipled in a life of walking and growing in that relationship. We believe that there are coaches and athletes that will accept the adventure (Lead Others) of developing their leadership skills in order to be a leader for Christ. We believe that healthy, loving relationships (Love Others) are also critical whether it is with family and friends or within the Church of Christ Simply put our Fundamentals can be defied as:

- **SHARE Him Boldly**
FCA shares Jesus with those who do not have a personal relationship with Him. We believe that salvation is only found in Jesus, and with great passion we desire to share the Gospel with the world. (Acts 5:42)
- **SEEK Him Passionately**
FCA equips and encourages others to seek Him daily. A life-long pursuit of knowing and loving Jesus takes perseverance and discipline. (Acts 17:11)
- **LEAD Others Faithfully**
FCA desires to model Jesus' example of serving by seeking out the needs of others, developing trusting relationships and caring about the individuals we serve.(1 Corinthians 14:12)
- **LOVE Others Unconditionally**
FCA realizes that the most powerful force in the world is love. We desire to be obedient to the Lord as He said that we would be known by our love. (1 Peter 4:8)

For more information or to contact FCA:
1-800-289-0909   www.FCA.org   fca@fca.org